THE SIMON EVANS BIOGRAPHY

Comedy Wordsmith-
Simon Evans and the Triumph of
Sophisticated Humor

Jennifer Moda

THE SIMON EVANS BIOGRAPHY

All rights reserved. Except in the case of quotation for specific reviews and other non-commercial uses allowed by copyright laws, no part of this publication may be Reproduced, recreated, distributed, or transmitted in any form or by any means, including recording, photocopying, or mechanical method, without the publisher's consent.

Copyright (2025) by Jennifer Moda

THE SIMON EVANS BIOGRAPHY

NOTICE OF DISCLAIMER

The content in this book is intended only as instructional. The author and publisher disclaim all expressed and implied representations and warranties regarding the availability, completeness, accuracy, reliability, suitability, or suitability of the content contained herein for any purpose, even though they have made every effort to present accurate and up-to-date information. Both the author and the publisher disclaim all liability for any loss or damage resulting from using this book, including but not limited to consequential or indirect loss or damage, or any loss or damage at all resulting from lost profits or data.

THE SIMON EVANS BIOGRAPHY

TABLE OF CONTENT

Introduction

Chapter One – Early Footsteps

Chapter Two – Finding His Voice

Chapter Three – Cutting His Teeth

Chapter Four – The Breakthrough

Chapter Five – The Comedian's Craft

Chapter Six – Beyond the Stage

Chapter Seven – Challenges and Triumphs

Chapter Eight – Legacy of Laughter

Conclusion

THE SIMON EVANS BIOGRAPHY

Introduction

In the crowded world of British stand-up comedy, where voices often blend and styles mimic one another, Simon Evans has always managed to sound unmistakably his own. He is the comedian who walks on stage with the quiet assurance of a man who has read more books than you, who has turned his life's experiences into sharp observations, and who wields a vocabulary so polished it could cut glass. Evans is not the kind of comic who needs to shout or wave his arms wildly for attention. Instead, he leans into his intelligence, his wit, and a style of delivery that seems effortless but is anything but accidental.

This biography is the story of how that voice was shaped — from the ordinary rhythms of a childhood in a modest English town to the extraordinary task of building a career in one of the most unforgiving professions: stand-up comedy. Along the way, Evans' journey tells us something about the persistence it takes to survive in comedy, the delicate balance between intellectual humor and broad appeal, and the way a performer can carve out a unique space even in a saturated landscape.

Simon Evans was never destined to become the kind of comedian who thrives on slapstick or shock value. From an early age, his sharp eye for human behavior and his love of language set him apart. In classrooms, he was more likely to be noticed for a clever aside than for mischief. At university, his fascination with culture and politics was already clear, and it provided fertile ground for the material that would later define his stage persona. His path to comedy wasn't a straight line, though; like many comics, he found himself taking detours through jobs and opportunities that didn't always make sense in the moment but eventually added depth to his perspective.

To understand Simon Evans, one must understand the peculiar world of the British comedy circuit in the late 1980s and 1990s, the era in which he began to cut his teeth. This was a scene where talent was measured in rooms above pubs, where comedians learned to survive in front of hostile or indifferent audiences, and where only the sharpest, most original voices rose above the noise. Evans emerged here not as a brash young firebrand but as a craftsman of carefully constructed routines, delivered with the poise of someone who believed words themselves were enough to hold attention.

Over time, his career moved beyond those small, smoky rooms. Evans became a familiar presence on radio, particularly through his long association with BBC Radio 4, where his programs and appearances showcased his ability to engage audiences in a different way. On radio, without the physical presence of a stage, he leaned even harder into the power of language, structure, and timing. His comedy was never about pratfalls or exaggerated personas — it was about clarity of thought sharpened into humor. In an age where comedy often risks collapsing into either raw confessional or blunt outrage, Evans provided a third path: comedy that was rigorous, elegant, and clever without being inaccessible.

THE SIMON EVANS BIOGRAPHY

This book explores not only the highlights of Simon Evans' professional life but also the struggles and setbacks that make his story compelling. Comedy is a precarious career at the best of times, and Evans has had to navigate the same uncertainties that every comic faces — inconsistent bookings, demanding audiences, the pressure to stay relevant. Yet through it all, he has held fast to a style that is distinctively his, proof that one doesn't have to abandon intellect or refinement in order to make people laugh.

Another layer of Evans' story lies in his refusal to be easily categorized. Some comedians are remembered primarily as satirists, others as storytellers, still others as clowns or provocateurs. Evans is harder to pin down. He is a satirist in the sense that he dissects culture and politics with a scalpel, but he is also a craftsman of language who seems almost literary at times. His stage presence carries an air of authority, yet it never strays into arrogance. He is capable of wry, personal storytelling without ever giving away more of himself than he chooses. This complexity is part of what makes his career worth telling — it is the story of a man who has built a niche not by chasing trends but by trusting in his own strengths.

Perhaps the most enduring quality of Simon Evans' comedy is that it respects the audience. He does not pander or simplify; he assumes that those listening are as capable of appreciating nuance as he is. In a world where comedians sometimes underestimate their crowds in pursuit of quick laughs, Evans insists on offering something richer. The result is comedy that lingers in the mind long after the show, comedy that rewards attention and invites thought as well as laughter.

The chapters that follow trace Simon Evans' journey from his earliest years through the defining moments of his career. They show us the boy who found joy in language, the young man testing his skills on uncertain stages, the comedian navigating the hazards of the circuit, and the established performer refining a voice that has become instantly recognizable. Along the way, we'll meet the influences, colleagues, and audiences that helped shape him, as well as the setbacks that forced him to adapt and grow.

At its core, though, this biography is about more than one man's career. It is about the art of comedy itself — what it asks of those who pursue it, and what it gives to those who succeed. Simon Evans' life offers a window into that art form: the long nights of preparation, the thrill of connecting with a crowd, the delicate balance of intellect and entertainment. Through his story, we are reminded that comedy is not simply about laughter but about connection, insight, and the courage to step into the spotlight armed with nothing but words.

Simon Evans has always been, in his own way, a quiet revolutionary in British comedy. Not by tearing down traditions, but by proving that tradition — the well-turned phrase, the carefully constructed argument, the dry wit delivered with perfect timing — still has power. His journey is proof that in comedy, as in life, sometimes the sharpest tools are not the loudest but the most precise.

THE SIMON EVANS BIOGRAPHY

This is his story.

Chapter One – Early Footsteps

Long before Simon Evans became the sharp-suited, sharp-tongued presence audiences across Britain came to admire, he was simply a boy growing up in the south of England with an ear for language and a restless curiosity about the world. His life in many ways did not scream "future comedian." There were no stories of the class clown disrupting lessons, no grand tales of teenage mischief designed to earn cheap laughs from his peers. Simon was quieter than that, more analytical. If anything, his early life was marked not by a craving for attention, but by an instinct to listen, to observe, to notice the subtleties of how people spoke and carried themselves. It was in those small observations, tucked away in his young mind, that the seeds of his comedy would eventually be planted.

Simon was born in 1965, a year that sat on the cusp of cultural transformation in Britain. The post-war decades had given rise to a world still defined by rationing memories and traditional values, but the sixties were also pulsing with change. By the time he was old enough to toddle around, the Beatles were dominating radio waves, satire was beginning to bite its way into mainstream entertainment, and the country was redefining itself. Growing up in this cultural swirl, Simon absorbed more than he probably realised. Comedy was beginning to shift from slapstick and music-hall to something sharper, more verbal, and his eventual style — dry,

THE SIMON EVANS BIOGRAPHY

intellectual, and incisive — would echo that cultural trajectory.

Family life in his childhood was not the stuff of spectacle but of steady influence. His father was practical, a man who appreciated order and discipline, while his mother carried a warmth and quiet wit that ran just below the surface. If Simon learned anything from her, it was that humor need not be loud to be effective. Sometimes a single raised eyebrow or a perfectly timed pause could say more than a flurry of words. Later, audiences would discover how much he relied on this principle: the power of timing, silence, and understatement.

Simon's schooling years offered fertile ground for his developing personality. He was a bright student, often more drawn to literature, history, and the art of argument than to the rigid logic of mathematics. Teachers noticed his aptitude for language, though perhaps not always his penchant for mischief. Rather than cracking jokes to derail a lesson, Simon preferred the wry remark, slipped in just under the radar, the kind that made a few pupils chuckle while leaving the teacher momentarily disarmed. He did not seek to dominate a room — he sought to bend it ever so slightly in his favor, to control the rhythm of conversation. It was a skill he would carry with him to the stage decades later.

Books were his constant companions. As other boys chased footballs across muddy fields, Simon often retreated to the world of ideas. He devoured the works of writers who mixed humor with intellect — George Orwell's sly political asides, Evelyn Waugh's biting satire, and later, the essays of people like Clive James, whose wit was a scalpel rather than a sledgehammer. He also tuned into the satirical voices that were beginning to dominate British radio and television, finding inspiration in the likes of *That Was the Week That Was* and, later, the sharp commentary of comedians who thrived on intelligence as much as performance.

Yet comedy was not an obvious career path for him. In fact, it was barely a path at all. As a teenager, Simon was far more focused on pursuing a stable, respectable trajectory. He flirted with the idea of academia, fascinated by the big questions of philosophy and the mechanics of society. University beckoned, and when he eventually arrived there, it provided him with both the intellectual challenge he craved and, unknowingly, the training ground for his comedy.

University life opened Simon up to a wider circle of voices and influences. The student bars and late-night debates over pints were fertile territory for testing his wit. Unlike the exaggerated clowning of some of his peers, his humor was precise, often delivered in the cadence of a barrister making his closing statement. He discovered that he could take apart an argument with a turn of phrase, expose absurdity with a carefully chosen metaphor. People began to notice: "You've got a way with words," friends would remark. He would laugh it off, but deep down he was beginning to sense that he had something unique.

Those early years also forged in Simon a taste for performance. He was not yet stepping on stage with a microphone, but he was learning the rhythm of an audience — whether it was a circle of friends gathered in a pub, or a seminar group waiting for someone to inject levity into a dry discussion. He learned how to hold a room, not by volume but by tone, pacing, and control. The seeds of Simon Evans the comedian were sprouting, even if he didn't yet recognize the crop he was planting.

It is worth noting that Evans' humor, even in its infancy, was never about slapstick or silliness. He was drawn instead to the absurdities of life's structure: the pomposity of institutions, the contradictions in middle-class life, the quirks of language. He once remarked in later years that comedy, for him, was not about telling jokes but about "drawing people's attention to the ridiculousness of things they hadn't considered ridiculous until you pointed it out." That sensibility was already there in his youth, simmering quietly, waiting for the right outlet.

By the time he left university, Simon Evans was armed with a sharp intellect, a growing sense of wit, and a nagging feeling that the conventional career paths laid before him might not suit. He dabbled in different jobs — journalism, copywriting, odd stints of writing work — each one sharpening his skills with words but leaving him unsatisfied. Something was missing, though he could not yet articulate what.

Looking back on those early footsteps, one can see how the disparate threads of his upbringing began to weave together into the tapestry of his future career. His quiet childhood had taught him observation. His academic years had trained his mind to dismantle ideas with precision. His fascination with literature and satire had given him a model for how humor could be both entertaining and intellectually nourishing. And the small, seemingly inconsequential moments — the sly remark in class, the barbed aside in a student debate, the quiet amusement at the absurdities of everyday life — had been rehearsals for the stage he would one day command.

There was also, hidden beneath it all, a stubbornness. Simon Evans was not a man destined to chase fame through cheap laughs. His comedy, when it came, would be crafted, thoughtful, and unapologetically intellectual. But in these early years, that stubborn streak showed itself in quieter ways: in his refusal to follow paths that didn't fit, in his determination to trust his instincts, and in his conviction that words — carefully chosen, precisely delivered — could reshape the way people thought and laughed.

The world of professional comedy still lay some years ahead. But the boy from the south of England, who grew up listening more than he spoke, reading more than he played, and watching more than he interrupted, was on his way. The early footsteps had been taken. What remained was to discover the road they were leading him toward.

Chapter Two – Finding His Voice

If Simon Evans' early life was marked by observation and quiet wit, his early adulthood was the point at which those instincts began to harden into something recognisably comic. Comedy had not yet announced itself as his destiny, but the building blocks were falling into place, each decision and detour shaping the voice he would eventually project on stage.

When Evans left university, he stepped into a world that demanded practicality. Like so many graduates, he found himself balancing lofty intellectual ambitions with the simple need to make a living. He dabbled in a range of jobs, some mundane, some more creatively demanding. Among them was copywriting — a field that suited his way with words but offered little satisfaction beyond the monthly paycheque. He could manipulate language, spin slogans, and craft clever headlines, but there was no spark, no sense that this was the arena where his wit could truly breathe.

What copywriting did provide, however, was discipline. Evans learned to respect structure, concision, and timing. Every advertisement had to grab attention in seconds, every line had to work doubly hard. These lessons would eventually echo in his comedy, where punchlines had to land with surgical precision and every extraneous word had to be pruned away. In a strange way, his time in the corporate world was an unintentional training ground for the rhythms of stand-up.

Still, something gnawed at him. He knew he wanted more than the nine-to-five treadmill. And so, like many restless young men of his generation, he turned toward creative outlets — writing projects, essays, occasional dabbling in performance. But it was not until he stumbled into the world of comedy clubs that his dormant instincts began to wake.

The British comedy circuit of the 1990s was a rough-and-ready place. Alternative comedy had exploded in the 1980s, tearing down the old order of mother-in-law jokes and tired stereotypes. In its place had risen a new kind of performer: raw, experimental, politically charged, sometimes anarchic. By the time Evans began haunting clubs and open-mic nights, the scene was still buzzing with that spirit of reinvention. It was a world that valued originality, intelligence, and voice above polish. And Evans, though still untested, had all three waiting in his arsenal.

His first forays onto the stage were tentative. Unlike some comedians who seemed to thrive on chaos, Evans carried himself with restraint. He was not the wide-eyed, frenetic type; he was measured, deliberate. His suits became part of his stage persona, a kind of visual shorthand for his brand of comedy: crisp, intellectual, a little aloof. Where other newcomers might have fumbled through stories, Evans spoke with clarity, often constructing his sets as though he were delivering a carefully reasoned argument in court.

The results were mixed at first. Audiences, accustomed to broader strokes, sometimes hesitated to catch the nuances of his wit. He was not trying to be slapstick-funny; he was trying to expose the absurdity of middle-class life, of politics, of everyday hypocrisies. But for those who listened closely, something clicked. A chuckle would ripple into laughter, and soon enough he would have the room leaning forward, eager to hear the next perfectly phrased dismantling of some cherished notion.

It was during this period that Evans began to truly "find his voice." He realised that his strength lay not in playing to the lowest common denominator but in trusting his audience to rise to his level. If a joke demanded knowledge of history, literature, or economics, so be it. If it required a longer setup before the payoff, he would take that risk. The audiences who stayed with him loved him for it, and slowly but surely,

THE SIMON EVANS BIOGRAPHY

word spread that Simon Evans was a comedian with a difference.

Of course, finding one's voice in comedy is rarely a smooth journey. Evans endured his share of brutal nights, when jokes fell flat and silence pressed in like a weight. In smoky clubs with sticky floors and audiences more interested in cheap beer than clever wordplay, he sometimes wondered if he had chosen the wrong path. But the failures were just as instructive as the triumphs. He learned resilience, the art of pivoting mid-set, the importance of reading a room. He toughened up, developing a professional armour that would later make him one of the most unflappable performers on the circuit.

THE SIMON EVANS BIOGRAPHY

By the late 1990s, Evans was beginning to carve out a place for himself. He was booked more regularly, climbing the ladder from small clubs to more respected venues. His style — equal parts witty barrister, mischievous professor, and wry social critic — began to crystallise. He wore his intelligence on his sleeve, but crucially, he wrapped it in warmth and humour rather than arrogance. Audiences did not feel lectured; they felt invited to share in the joke, even when it required them to think.

During these years, Evans also made his first ventures into broadcasting. Radio in particular suited him. On BBC Radio 4, his measured voice and articulate style felt at home. Unlike the brashness of some television comedy, radio allowed for nuance, for longer narratives, for jokes that could build over paragraphs rather than seconds. Shows like *The News Quiz* and *The Now Show* provided him a platform to refine his craft in front of wider audiences, and listeners quickly recognised that he was not just another comic voice — he was a writer, a thinker, a satirist.

Perhaps the most significant development in this period, however, was his growing confidence in his own comedic worldview. Evans realised that he was at his best when he leaned into who he truly was: middle-aged, middle-class, articulate, slightly pompous but entirely self-aware. He mined this persona for gold, gently mocking himself even as he skewered the society around him. His routines about family life, social conventions, and the peculiarities of modern Britain struck a chord. People saw themselves in his jokes — their frustrations, their hypocrisies, their small triumphs.

Behind the scenes, Evans was also discovering the balancing act of a comedian's life. Touring meant long nights, endless travel, and the constant uncertainty of live performance. There was little glamour in the early years — cheap motels, late trains, and the perpetual hustle of chasing the next gig. But for all its grind, comedy gave him something that no other job had offered: purpose. For the first time, Evans felt that his love of words, his knack for observation, and his instinct for timing had found their rightful stage.

By the turn of the millennium, Simon Evans was no longer a hopeful newcomer but a recognised voice in the British comedy landscape. He had not yet reached the mainstream fame of panel shows and national tours, but he had built a foundation. More importantly, he had discovered the essence of his comedic identity: intelligent without being inaccessible, cutting without being cruel, refined without being dull.

Finding his voice had not been about inventing a character but about uncovering the one that had been there all along. The quiet boy who once listened more than he spoke had become the man who commanded rooms with carefully chosen words. The student who relished debate had become the performer who thrived on dismantling arguments with humour. And the restless young professional who once drifted through unsatisfying jobs had become the comedian who finally knew where he belonged.

THE SIMON EVANS BIOGRAPHY

Simon Evans was on his way. The next chapter of his career — the breakthrough into wider recognition, television, and the national stage — awaited him. But he would never forget those early gigs, the small audiences, the hard lessons, and the thrill of finding his voice for the first time.

THE SIMON EVANS BIOGRAPHY

Chapter Three – Cutting His Teeth

Every comedian who makes it onto a stage large enough to draw cameras and ticket-paying crowds has endured the long apprenticeship of the circuit. For Simon Evans, those years were not just a testing ground — they were a crucible. It was here, in the cramped clubs and regional theatres of Britain, that he hammered his intellect and wit into a finely tuned instrument. If Chapter Two had been about finding his voice, Chapter Three was about sharpening it until it gleamed.

The late 1990s and early 2000s were a boom time for stand-up in the UK. Comedy clubs had sprung up across the country, and audiences were hungry for live laughter. At the same time, the alternative comedy explosion of the previous decade had loosened the rules. Comedians no longer had to mimic the working men's club patter of old. They could be political, surreal, observational, personal — or, in Evans' case, intellectual and satirical. The field was wide open, but that did not mean the competition was easy. If anything, it was fiercer than ever.

Evans entered this world with a style that was unusual for the circuit. He didn't shout, he didn't posture, and he certainly didn't pander. Instead, he strolled onstage in a suit — crisp shirt, tie neatly knotted — and delivered his routines with the air of a QC presenting evidence to a jury. At first, some audiences weren't sure what to make of him. "Who's this posh bloke?" you could almost hear them mutter. But then the jokes would land, perfectly balanced between cutting observation and sly self-deprecation, and soon enough the laughter would break through.

What set Evans apart was not just his delivery, but his craftsmanship. He worked tirelessly on his material, editing and re-editing until every phrase carried its weight. He once described writing comedy as "akin to engineering — remove the unnecessary, reinforce the structure, ensure it will hold under pressure." On the circuit, this perfectionism paid dividends. While some comedians coasted on charisma, Evans built routines that could withstand the scrutiny of any audience.

The road was not glamorous. He played pubs in front of half-drunk patrons, tiny upstairs rooms where the ceiling fans clattered louder than the laughter, and provincial theatres where the smell of stale beer clung to the curtains. There were nights when he killed, and nights when he bombed. But Evans treated each gig as part of his apprenticeship. If a line didn't land, he asked himself why. If a routine soared, he dissected what made it work. In those years, he was both performer and scientist, forever testing hypotheses about human behavior and humor.

Other comedians on the circuit began to take notice. Evans wasn't the loudest act, but he was among the most consistent. His dry wit and articulate style earned him respect from his peers, even if he wasn't always the crowd favorite in rowdy clubs. He was, in many ways, a comedian's comedian — someone other performers admired for his craftsmanship and intelligence.

But the circuit was not just about honing material. It was also about survival. Long drives up and down the country, late-night trains, cheap lodgings, and endless takeaway meals took their toll. Evans, with his meticulous nature, approached the grind with stoic professionalism. He kept notebooks filled with routines, observations, and fragments of dialogue overheard in train carriages or service stations. His comedy was rooted in real life, and the endless travel provided him with a constant stream of material.

It was during this period that Evans began to develop the themes that would become his hallmark. He found comedy gold in middle-class anxieties — the petty rivalries of suburbia, the absurdities of parenting, the contradictions of modern liberalism. He also turned his gaze to politics, skewering both left and right with equal relish. His routines were not sermons, but they were undeniably intelligent, and audiences who leaned in to catch the subtleties found themselves richly rewarded.

Television opportunities began to trickle in. Evans' first appearances on panel shows and comedy showcases were tentative steps into the mainstream. The format suited him: quick-witted exchanges, verbal jousts, the chance to deliver finely honed one-liners. Shows like *Have I Got News for You and Mock the Week prized the ability to think fast, and Evans' sharp mind was more than up to the challenge. Radio too remained a faithful ally. On The News Quiz. and The Now Show, his voice carried authority, his jokes landing with the weight of reasoned argument.

Still, breaking through to wider recognition was no easy task. Evans was competing against louder, brasher acts whose styles often played better on television. His comedy demanded attention — it required audiences to listen carefully — and in the age of quick soundbites, that was sometimes a harder sell. Yet he refused to compromise his voice. Where others chased trends, Evans doubled down on being himself. That stubbornness, which had once made him restless in ordinary jobs, now became his greatest asset.

By the early 2000s, Evans was not only respected but also increasingly in demand. He toured more extensively, moving from club sets to full solo shows. Edinburgh, with its sprawling Fringe Festival, became a proving ground. His shows there revealed him as more than a gag merchant; they showcased his ability to weave longer narratives, to build themes that carried audiences through an entire hour of comedy. Critics began to take note, praising his intelligence and polish.

But it wasn't just critics. Audiences were beginning to claim him as their own. For those who felt alienated by comedy that was too crude or too chaotic, Evans offered something different: wit with substance, humor with bite, laughter that left you thinking as well as chuckling. He filled a niche that no one else quite occupied, and in doing so, he began to carve out his legacy.

Of course, the road was not without its stumbles. Comedy is a brutal business, and even seasoned

THE SIMON EVANS BIOGRAPHY

performers endure nights of failure. Evans had them too — nights when his carefully crafted jokes met with blank stares or, worse, heckles. Yet even here, his style worked to his advantage. Where some comedians bristled or lashed out, Evans parried with wit, treating hecklers as though they were foolish opponents in a debate. More often than not, he emerged victorious, winning the room back with a single devastating put-down delivered in his calm, lawyerly cadence.

As the 2000s unfolded, Evans' reputation grew. He was no longer merely cutting his teeth — he had become a fixture of the circuit, a reliable draw, a comedian whose name carried weight. His voice had matured, his material had deepened, and his confidence on stage was unshakeable. He was not yet a household name, but within the world of British comedy, Simon Evans was a force to be reckoned with.

Looking back on those years, Evans would later describe them as both grueling and exhilarating. They were the years when he learned not just how to tell jokes, but how to *be* a comedian — how to own a stage, connect with an audience, and turn observation into art. The circuit had tested him, shaped him, and ultimately, prepared him for the bigger stages to come.

Simon Evans had cut his teeth. Now he was ready to bite.

Chapter Four – The Breakthrough

For every comedian who endures the grind of the circuit, there comes a moment — or rather, a series of moments — when the balance tips. The years of small audiences, late trains, and jokes that sometimes died in the air begin to yield to something larger: recognition. For Simon Evans, that breakthrough came not in a single blinding flash of fame, but as a steady accumulation of appearances, reviews, and word-of-mouth momentum that gradually elevated him from "comedian's comedian" to one of the most respected voices in British stand-up.

By the mid-2000s, Evans had built a formidable reputation on the live circuit. His solo shows at the Edinburgh Festival Fringe had grown steadily in confidence and ambition. No longer just a performer testing routines in twenty-minute club slots, Evans was delivering full-length shows that revealed him as a craftsman with something distinctive to say. Edinburgh, with its frenetic energy and endless competition, was a ruthless testing ground. Yet Evans' polished style cut through the chaos. Critics began to note his command of language, his deft timing, and his willingness to take audiences on intellectual detours that few other comedians dared attempt.

What set him apart was not simply the content of his jokes, but the way he positioned himself on stage. Evans leaned fully into his persona as the sharp-suited, middle-class satirist — the man who appeared as though he had just stepped out of a debating chamber and wandered into a

THE SIMON EVANS BIOGRAPHY

comedy club by mistake. The choice was deliberate. In a comedy landscape often dominated by the casual, the scruffy, and the self-deprecating, Evans projected control, intellect, and a touch of pomposity. And because he was so adept at undercutting himself, audiences were drawn in rather than alienated.

The television industry soon came calling. Panel shows, which had become a major gateway for comedians into the mainstream, proved to be a natural fit. Evans' first significant appearances on Mock the Week and Have I Got News for You showcased his quick wit and ability to joust verbally with some of the sharpest comics in the country. Where others competed for airtime with noise and volume, Evans relied on precision. A single well-placed remark could cut through the chatter and earn a roomful of laughter. Viewers at home began to take note: here was a comedian with the bearing of a barrister and the sting of a satirist.

Radio, however, remained his most natural platform. On BBC Radio 4, Evans' voice carried the authority of a seasoned raconteur. He became a regular presence on The News Quiz and The Now Show, where his articulate monologues stood out for their blend of wit and reason. He also developed his own series, Simon Evans Goes to Market, which explored the world of economics through comedy. The show was emblematic of what made Evans unique: he could take subjects that might seem dry or inaccessible and render them hilarious without diluting their complexity. Audiences who might have tuned in expecting an easy laugh instead found themselves both entertained and educated — a hallmark of Evans' style.

With each new platform, Evans' audience grew. Fans who had first encountered him in a small club now saw him on television; radio listeners discovered him live at festivals; critics began to hail him as one of the sharpest minds in comedy. Yet through it all, Evans maintained the meticulous craftsmanship that had defined his career from the start. He was never one to coast on reputation. Every show was rewritten, every joke scrutinised, every performance treated as an opportunity to refine his art.

The "breakthrough," then, was not a sudden eruption but a gradual unfolding. By the late 2000s, Evans was selling out theatres, headlining tours, and establishing himself as a fixture on the national scene. He had moved beyond being simply respected within the circuit; he had become a recognisable name to the wider public. His comedy albums and DVDs found audiences eager to revisit his work, and his live tours confirmed his ability to hold a room for ninety minutes without flagging.

What truly solidified Evans' place in the comedy world, however, was his consistency. In an industry that often rewards novelty, Evans built a reputation on reliability. Audiences who bought tickets to see him knew what they were getting: intelligence, polish, and laughs that carried substance. He was not a comedian chasing viral moments or gimmicks; he was a craftsman delivering a body of work that would endure.

And yet, despite the breakthrough into wider recognition, Evans never lost sight of the grind that had brought him there. He continued to play smaller venues, testing new material, staying connected to the roots of stand-up. To him, the circuit was not something to be escaped, but something to be honoured. It was the laboratory where jokes were forged, the proving ground where comedians earned their stripes. Even as his profile grew, he returned to those rooms, sharp suit and all, to ensure his comedy never drifted from its source.

The breakthrough years also coincided with shifts in Evans' personal life. Fatherhood added new dimensions to his material. His routines about the trials of parenting resonated with audiences who recognised their own struggles in his dry, self-mocking anecdotes. The once aloof, slightly pompous stage persona now carried a humanising warmth — the middle-aged father grappling with school runs, family holidays, and the slow erosion of dignity at the hands of one's own children. This new layer of relatability deepened his connection with audiences and broadened his appeal beyond the intellectual niche.

By the end of the 2000s, Simon Evans was firmly established as one of Britain's most distinctive comedic voices. He had not taken the easiest path, nor the fastest, but his breakthrough was all the more enduring because of it. He had built his reputation brick by brick, joke by joke, gig by gig, until the edifice was strong enough to withstand the fickle winds of the entertainment industry.

THE SIMON EVANS BIOGRAPHY

For Evans, the real reward of the breakthrough was not fame — though recognition certainly made life more comfortable — but the freedom it afforded. He could now craft shows on his own terms, explore subjects that fascinated him, and trust that his audience would follow. Comedy, once a precarious hustle, had become a sustainable career, a platform for his voice, and a legacy in the making.

The boy who had once sat quietly observing others had become the man who commanded stages and airwaves across the nation. The breakthrough had arrived, not as a flash in the pan, but as the culmination of years of craft, persistence, and unwavering belief in his unique voice.

THE SIMON EVANS BIOGRAPHY

Simon Evans was no longer cutting his teeth. He was biting into the mainstream — and leaving a mark.

Chapter Five – The Comedian's Craft

By the time Simon Evans had broken into the mainstream, one thing had become abundantly clear to anyone who watched him work: he was not merely a comedian; he was a craftsman. Where many comics relied on instinct, improvisation, or sheer personality, Evans treated comedy as both an art and a science. Every pause, every inflection, every syllable of his delivery was considered, measured, and honed. To truly understand Simon Evans, one had to understand the meticulous process behind the laughter.

Evans' comedy was built on language. He was, at his core, a wordsmith. He loved the way words could dance, collide, and undercut each other. His notebooks were filled not just with punchlines but with fragments of phrases, alternative synonyms, and careful rearrangements. He once compared writing comedy to carpentry: "You can't just throw together a few planks and call it a table. It has to stand up, it has to support weight, it has to be elegant. And it shouldn't have any unnecessary screws sticking out." That philosophy guided his approach to every set he constructed.

Unlike comedians who thrived on chaos or spontaneity, Evans thrived on structure. His routines often resembled arguments — a claim presented, examined, dismantled, and rebuilt — with the audience as the jury. His punchlines arrived not as random surprises but as logical conclusions, often so inevitable in hindsight that audiences laughed as much at their own recognition as at the joke itself. This intellectual rigour gave his comedy a unique texture: it was laughter grounded in reason, humour born of logic.

But if his craft was disciplined, it was never sterile. Evans understood the alchemy of performance. Timing was everything. He had an almost musical sense of rhythm, knowing exactly when to allow silence to stretch and when to cut it off with a sharp line. His pauses were weapons, as potent as his words. A raised eyebrow, a slight tilt of the head, a carefully deployed sigh — these gestures carried as much weight as his meticulously polished sentences.

One of Evans' greatest strengths was his ability to build tension. He would often begin a routine in a seemingly mundane place — a story about family life, a passing observation about politics, a quirk of middle-class living. Slowly, he would layer detail upon detail, drawing the audience into his web. Just when they thought they knew where he was going, he would pivot, exposing the absurdity beneath the surface. The release, when it came, was cathartic. Audiences roared not just because the line was funny, but because they had been guided there so expertly.

The themes of Evans' comedy also spoke to his craft. He had no interest in easy targets or throwaway gags. His routines often grappled with weighty subjects — economics, politics, the contradictions of modern liberalism, the hypocrisies of middle-class life. His BBC Radio 4 series Simon Evans Goes to Market exemplified this approach. Each episode took a complex economic concept — inflation, commodities, the housing market — and broke it down with humour. Evans never dumbed the material down; he trusted his audience to keep up. In doing so, he carved a niche unlike any other comedian of his generation: intellectual comedy that was genuinely funny.

And yet, for all his cerebral material, Evans never drifted too far from the personal. His routines about family life, particularly about being a middle-aged father, were some of his most beloved. He mined the absurdities of parenthood with the same precision he applied to economics, exposing the indignities of middle age and the relentless march of domestic chaos. These routines softened his otherwise formal persona, grounding him in experiences audiences recognised instantly. They revealed the heart beneath the intellect, the warmth beneath the wit.

Craft, for Evans, extended beyond writing and delivery. He was equally disciplined about performance. He approached each gig as a professional engagement, arriving prepared, suited, and focused. While some comedians leaned on the casual aesthetic of jeans and t-shirts, Evans' formal attire was part of his art. The suit was not a costume; it was a signal. It told the audience that this man took his craft seriously, that what they were about to hear had been thought through, sharpened, and polished. It also provided a useful layer of irony: the buttoned-up, serious figure delivering razor-sharp comedy about the very world he appeared to embody.

THE SIMON EVANS BIOGRAPHY

This duality — the serious exterior concealing a mischievous wit — became central to his craft. Audiences laughed not just at what he said, but at the incongruity of how he said it. Evans could dismantle a government policy with the tone of a civil servant drafting a memo, or describe the trials of fatherhood as though he were presenting evidence in court. The form and the content worked in tandem, each enhancing the other.

Colleagues in the comedy world often spoke of Evans' relentless work ethic. He was not the type to dash off material on the way to a gig. He rewrote, rehearsed, and refined. He tested material in smaller clubs, adjusted it based on audience response, and only then integrated it into larger shows. His Edinburgh Fringe performances were legendary for their polish, each one the product of months of preparation.

Where others relied on charm to carry them through rough patches, Evans relied on precision.

But precision did not mean rigidity. One of the hallmarks of Evans' craft was his ability to respond to the room. He was a master of handling hecklers, not with aggression but with wit. When challenged, he never lost composure; instead, he dismantled his interrupters with the same calm logic he applied to his routines. A heckler might begin with bravado, only to find themselves gently but devastatingly reduced to silence by Evans' sharp tongue. These moments became part of his legend, reinforcing his reputation as a comedian who could handle anything thrown his way.

THE SIMON EVANS BIOGRAPHY

Another element of his craft was his refusal to pander. Evans never chased trends or watered down his material for mass appeal. He trusted his audience to meet him where he stood. If a joke required knowledge of literature, history, or politics, he delivered it without apology. This faith in his audience was not arrogance but respect. He believed comedy could be both entertaining and enriching, and his fans loved him for it. They came not just to laugh, but to be challenged, to feel part of something smarter than the average gag.

Over time, Evans' approach to craft also became part of his identity within the comedy world. He was not the wild improviser, the slapstick clown, or the controversial shock-jock. He was the craftsman — the comedian who treated his work with the seriousness of an artisan perfecting a violin. His comedy was built to last, to be revisited, to reward careful listening.

Yet for all the polish, Evans never lost sight of the essential truth of his craft: comedy, at its core, was about connection. His meticulous preparation was not about showing off intellect but about ensuring the audience had the best possible experience. He respected the transaction at the heart of live performance: people had given him their time and attention, and he owed them laughter in return. That sense of responsibility, more than anything else, defined his approach.

By the late 2010s, Simon Evans had become synonymous with high-calibre, intelligent stand-up. Critics praised his craftsmanship; fellow comedians admired his discipline;

audiences trusted him to deliver. He had carved out a unique space in British comedy — one where wit and intellect lived comfortably alongside warmth and relatability.

The craft was never finished, of course. Each new show brought fresh challenges, each tour new lessons. But by this stage of his career, Evans had built a body of work that stood as a testament to his philosophy: that comedy could be both clever and hilarious, both precise and human, both crafted and alive.

And for Simon Evans, that was the point. Comedy was not about chasing laughs at any cost. It was about building something solid, something true, something that would last long after the applause had faded.

Chapter Six – Beyond the Stage

For many comedians, the stage is both the battlefield and the sanctuary — the one place where all their anxieties and frustrations can be transformed into laughter. For Simon Evans, however, comedy was never just about the moment of performance under the hot lights. As his career unfolded, it became increasingly clear that his wit, intellect, and unique voice extended far beyond the comedy club. Radio, television, writing, and even the role of cultural commentator beckoned. Each medium offered Evans a new canvas, and he approached them all with the same mix of sharp intelligence and dry detachment that had won him acclaim as a stand-up.

THE SIMON EVANS BIOGRAPHY

By the late 2000s, Evans had already established himself as a familiar face on the UK comedy circuit. His reputation as a comic who could weave articulate, almost literary routines around social and political themes had made him a reliable booking. But it was on the airwaves, particularly with the BBC, that Evans began to reach audiences who had never set foot inside a comedy club. Radio — that most deceptively intimate of mediums — became his second stage.

Finding His Voice on Radio

BBC Radio 4, the hallowed home of British intellectual humor, became the natural environment for Evans. His voice — calm, deliberate, and tinged with irony — seemed tailor-made for the medium. His appearances on panel shows such as *The News Quiz* and *The Unbelievable Truth* allowed him to demonstrate what many live audiences already knew: that his comedy was not just funny but thought-provoking. He relished the chance to engage with contemporary issues, not in the shouty, aggressive style of some of his peers, but with a cool precision.

Evans' presence on Radio 4 grew to the point where he was entrusted with his own series: *Simon Evans Goes to Market*. Launched in 2014, the program explored the history, psychology, and human impact of economics — a subject that might seem dry or forbidding in the wrong hands. Yet Evans treated it with a blend of academic rigor and comic flair. One episode might examine the rise of tulip mania in 17th-century Holland, another the psychology behind modern stock exchanges. Through it all, Evans maintained his comic's instinct for the absurd, finding humor in the way money shapes our desires and delusions.

The show was not merely a comedy vehicle; it was a genuine exploration of ideas, introducing listeners to economic principles through the prism of jokes and anecdotes. Critics praised Evans for managing a rare feat: making economics entertaining without dumbing it down. In this respect, the series was a microcosm of his broader career. Evans had long rejected the idea that comedy had to pander to the lowest common denominator. Instead, he seemed to take pride in challenging his audiences, whether they were sitting in a radio studio or a theatre.

THE SIMON EVANS BIOGRAPHY

Television: A Sharper Spotlight

If radio allowed Evans to showcase his intellect, television put his persona in sharper relief. His appearances on shows like *Mock the Week*, Live at the Apollo, and Michael McIntyre's Comedy Roadshow introduced him to a broader audience. Here, the stakes were higher — television was a crowded space where comics fought for airtime, often reducing their material to quick gags or eye-catching antics.

Evans, however, remained true to his style. His performances on *Live at the Apollo*, for example, were studies in precision. Dressed in his trademark suit, he cut the figure of a wry, world-weary intellectual, bemused by the modern world. The contrast with other comics — often younger, brasher, or more physical —

only heightened the distinctiveness of his approach. Evans was not there to bound across the stage or to charm with puppyish enthusiasm. He was there to dissect society with a scalpel, and he did so with impeccable timing.

Television also exposed Evans to the peculiar pressures of mass entertainment. In the studio, his carefully constructed routines sometimes had to be trimmed for time, and the demands of editing could disrupt his narrative style. Yet he managed to adapt, honing his material into compact bursts of wit that still conveyed his worldview. Though he never became a fixture of television in the way some of his contemporaries did, his appearances cemented his reputation as a comic who could hold his own in any setting.

The Writer Behind the Comic

THE SIMON EVANS BIOGRAPHY

While audiences often know comedians only through their stage presence, much of the work happens off-stage — in solitude, at the desk, with a notebook or laptop. Evans' career as a writer paralleled his performing life. He contributed material not only for his own shows but also for other comedians and radio projects.

Writing was where Evans' love of language came to the fore. His sentences, even in casual conversation, bore the marks of careful construction — subordinate clauses nestled within main ideas, jokes layered with irony and reference. This literary bent allowed him to thrive in formats that relied heavily on the written word, such as radio monologues or scripted panel contributions.

His role as a writer also extended to social commentary. In essays, columns, and occasional interviews, Evans would address cultural issues with the same unsparing eye he brought to comedy. He often positioned himself as a skeptic of fashionable ideas, preferring to question orthodoxies rather than reinforce them. This sometimes brought him into tension with the more progressive corners of the comedy world, but it also earned him admiration from audiences who appreciated his refusal to toe any party line.

A Cultural Commentator

As his career evolved, Evans increasingly found himself cast not just as a comedian but as a commentator on British life. His routines on wealth, class, and politics resonated with audiences who sensed that beneath the jokes lay a serious critique. Unlike some comedians who wore their political leanings on their sleeves, Evans played the contrarian, questioning both left and right with equal disdain.

This role as cultural gadfly was amplified by the rise of podcasts and digital platforms, which gave Evans new outlets for his ideas. He was invited onto discussion shows where comedy and commentary blurred, and his knack for articulating complex issues in a witty but accessible way made him a popular guest.

In interviews, Evans sometimes reflected on the peculiar position of comedians in public life. Were they merely jesters, licensed to mock but not to be taken seriously? Or had they, in the age of satire and political comedy, become a kind of alternative priesthood, offering moral insight under the cover of humor? Evans seemed skeptical of both extremes. To him, comedy was neither trivial nor sacred. It was, at its best, a form of truth-telling — but one that worked precisely because it avoided the sanctimony of politics or philosophy.

Balancing Persona and Person

As Evans' profile grew, so did the curiosity about the man behind the mic. Interviews often revealed a more reflective figure than his stage persona suggested. He was candid about the challenges of sustaining a comedy career, the uncertainties of freelance life, and the personal sacrifices required.

At the same time, Evans was careful not to indulge in too much self-revelation. Unlike some comedians who mined their personal lives for material, Evans tended to keep a certain distance between his private self and his public performances. This reserve contributed to his air of authority; he appeared less as a confessional storyteller than as a sardonic observer, the voice in the corner pointing out the absurdity of the world.

The Broader Impact

Looking back at Evans' ventures beyond the stage, one sees not a detour but an expansion of his comic identity. Radio gave him the chance to be both teacher and entertainer. Television showcased his ability to adapt his routines for mainstream audiences. Writing allowed him to refine his voice and explore subjects that resisted punchlines. And his role as cultural commentator positioned him as a thinker as well as a performer.

What united these diverse activities was a consistent sensibility: skeptical, articulate, and dryly amused by human folly. Whether he was explaining economic bubbles, trading quips on a panel show, or writing a column on social trends, Evans maintained the same commitment to clarity and wit.

Beyond the Stage, But Always a Comedian

Even as Evans embraced these broader roles, the stage remained central. He often noted that live performance provided an irreplaceable feedback loop, a reminder that comedy was ultimately about human connection. Yet the fact that he could succeed in so many other formats spoke to the depth of his talent.

For Simon Evans, comedy was never just a job or a performance style. It was a lens — a way of looking at the world that could be applied in a theatre, a radio studio, or a newspaper column. Beyond the stage, he was still very much a comedian, though one whose intellect and curiosity led him into unexpected places.

And in those places — whether economics, politics, or cultural debate — Evans proved that laughter and learning need not be opposites. They could, in the right hands, be one and the same.

Chapter Seven – Challenges and Triumphs

Success in comedy, much like in life, is rarely a smooth ascent. For Simon Evans, the climb had always been steep, filled with sharp edges of irony that suited his comedic temperament. But as his profile grew, so too did the weight of expectation. The man who had once been content to deliver barbed observations in the smoky backrooms of Britain's comedy clubs found himself facing an altogether different test: the demands of longevity in a career that thrives on reinvention, resilience, and risk.

By the late 2000s, Simon Evans was a familiar face on the circuit, a recognized voice on Radio 4, and an established act at Edinburgh. He had achieved the elusive badge of being "known" in comedy without crossing fully into celebrity. To some, that was a blessing — no paparazzi to stalk his home, no tabloid headlines about his private life — but it was also a source of quiet frustration. He was admired, respected, even beloved in certain circles, yet not universally recognized. Comedy, as Simon often reflected, is a trade where being overlooked can sting just as much as being criticized.

It was around this time that Evans began to feel the tension between his comedic persona and the ever-shifting landscape of the industry. Stand-up, once the bastion of intellectual subversion, was increasingly merging with the world of social media soundbites, panel-show banter, and twenty-second clips designed to go viral. For a comedian like Simon, who built routines meticulously, with layers of irony and tightly constructed arguments, this cultural shift posed a real challenge. "I'm not sure my material lends itself to TikTok," he joked in one interview, though beneath the wit lay a genuine unease about where comedy was heading.

Another challenge emerged in the form of cultural politics. Simon's comedy had always leaned on his ability to articulate what many felt but few dared to say — the hypocrisies of middle-class life, the contradictions of modern Britain, the peculiarities of political correctness. His delivery was calm, even scholarly, but the ideas behind the jokes sometimes brushed against the raw nerves of a society growing more polarized by the day. Inevitably, he found himself at the center of debates about free speech and comedy's role in public discourse.

THE SIMON EVANS BIOGRAPHY

For some critics, Simon's work carried a reactionary edge; for others, it was a refreshing antidote to what they saw as the homogenization of stand-up. He himself dismissed such labels, pointing out that comedy was, and should always be, a space where ideas could be tested in the crucible of laughter. "I don't write jokes to be applauded," he once remarked, "I write them to be laughed at. The applause is just collateral." Still, the tension gnawed at him. In private, Simon admitted that the pressure to both push boundaries and avoid missteps was one of the trickiest parts of his career.

It wasn't only cultural headwinds that tested him. The life of a touring comedian, even a successful one, is riddled with exhaustion. Endless travel, hotel rooms that all look the same, and nights spent in the adrenaline-high of performance followed by the crash of solitude. For Simon, who prided himself on balance and family life, these challenges took a toll. He was married with children, and though he cherished his role as a father, the demands of comedy often pulled him away from home at the very moments he wanted to be most present. In interviews, he has spoken candidly about this struggle, admitting that comedy is "a selfish profession, because the audience only sees you at your best, while your family sees the cost of that performance."

And then, like for so many others, came 2020. The global pandemic hit live comedy with brutal force, silencing venues, shuttering festivals, and pulling the rug from under comedians worldwide. Simon's tour dates were canceled overnight. Gigs that had taken months to book vanished in an instant. For a performer whose livelihood depended on live audiences, the situation was dire. Some comedians adapted quickly, streaming sets online, performing in drive-in theatres, or pivoting to podcasts. But for Simon, whose strength lay in the charged, immediate connection of live wit, the digital alternatives felt hollow. "Comedy without an audience is like tennis without a net," he quipped, summing up the frustration of trying to generate energy without the feedback loop of laughter.

Yet even in adversity, Simon Evans found a way forward. He turned to radio, a medium that had always embraced his style of comedy. His show *Simon Evans Goes to Market*, which had debuted years earlier, became a touchstone once again — a clever blend of economics, humor,

THE SIMON EVANS BIOGRAPHY

and social observation. During lockdown, audiences leaned on the familiar comfort of Radio 4, and Simon's erudite yet playful voice provided both entertainment and insight. The show reminded listeners that comedy could be as cerebral as it was funny, and it reinforced his place as one of Britain's most articulate comics.

This period also gave Simon time to reflect. For years, he had been caught in the relentless churn of gigging, touring, and writing. Suddenly forced into stillness, he reassessed not only his career but his life. He read voraciously, tinkered with new material, and began sketching out ideas that might not have fit the frenetic pace of pre-pandemic comedy. In hindsight, he described this pause as both terrifying and liberating — a disruption that shook his foundations but also reminded him why he had chosen comedy in the first place.

When live shows eventually returned, Simon emerged with renewed vigor. His material carried a sharper edge, honed by months of reflection, and audiences responded. The hunger for live performance was palpable, and Simon's thoughtful, carefully wrought routines stood out in a scene that was, in some quarters, saturated with hastily cobbled pandemic jokes. His comeback performances were hailed as some of his strongest in years.

But perhaps his greatest triumph during this period was not on stage but in his quiet persistence. Many comedians saw their careers derailed entirely by the pandemic. Others burned out in the struggle to adapt. Simon Evans, however, weathered the storm not by reinventing himself as something he wasn't, but by doubling down on who he was: a comedian who valued craft, precision, and integrity.

As he entered the next phase of his career, Simon began to think more about his legacy. He had never been the household name of certain contemporaries, but he had built something arguably more enduring: a body of work respected across generations of comedians, admired by critics, and cherished by audiences who sought comedy that respected their intelligence.

The triumphs, then, were not the flashy victories of celebrity or fortune but the quieter successes of authenticity. Simon Evans remained true to his voice in a profession that often rewards those who bend to trends. He navigated cultural debates without losing his balance, survived the industry's greatest disruption in living memory, and continued to write and perform with the same meticulous care that had defined his early years.

Looking back, Evans himself might joke that the greatest triumph of his career was simply surviving it — not because it had been joyless, but because survival in comedy is no small feat. To endure, to still be relevant, to still be funny after decades in a business that chews up talent and discards it with alarming speed — that was the real victory.

As Simon prepared for the future, the challenges were far from over. Comedy would continue to evolve, audiences would continue to change, and the cultural tides would ebb and flow. But if his journey had taught him anything, it was that laughter, when rooted in truth and intelligence, will always find its place.

And so, Simon Evans — the bespectacled, sharp-tongued, quietly rebellious craftsman of comedy — stood at a place where he could both reflect and look forward. He had been tested, more than once, but each challenge had left him not diminished but sharpened, more resolute, more certain of his place in the unpredictable, exhilarating world of stand-up.

Chapter Eight – Legacy of Laughter

In the dimly lit theatres and packed radio studios where Simon Evans has made his mark, laughter has always been the currency. But for Evans, laughter was never just a reflex — it was a bridge. A bridge between the intellect and the heart, between politics and personality, between the everyday frustrations of modern Britain and the timeless quirks of human behavior. To understand his legacy, one has to trace not only the arc of his career but also the way his comedy reshaped conversations, nudged boundaries, and left audiences thinking as much as they laughed.

By the late 2010s, Evans was no longer just "that sharp comedian" who popped up on BBC panel shows or the voice that punctuated Radio 4's

THE SIMON EVANS BIOGRAPHY

comedy schedule. He had become a touchstone in British stand-up — a figure audiences associated with wit laced with intelligence, a performer who could draw out laughs not by descending into slapstick or shock but by coaxing his listeners into joining him on a mental journey. This was perhaps his greatest gift: his ability to make an audience feel cleverer for having listened to him.

Comedy is often measured in applause and ticket sales, but Evans' impact was subtler, more enduring. He came to embody the idea that stand-up could be sophisticated without being elitist. In an age when many comedians leaned on self-deprecation or the comfort of universal, safe topics, Evans chose to court complexity. He talked about economics, philosophy, the changing dynamics of class — areas more commonly reserved for late-night documentaries than comedy clubs. Yet somehow, when filtered through his lens, these themes felt approachable, even exhilarating.

One particular example stands out in the collective memory of fans: his show Genius on Radio 4, where his crisp delivery turned what could have been dry debate into something electric. There was always a sharpness to his perspective, but it never came across as cruel. His humor had teeth, but they weren't there to wound — they were there to slice through pretension, to puncture bubbles of complacency. That balance — satirical without being sneering — became a hallmark of his style.

As Evans' reputation grew, younger comedians began citing him as an influence. They admired not only his craft but also his commitment to the craft. He wasn't one to chase trends or dilute his material for cheap applause. Instead, he maintained a consistency of voice that gave his work a timelessness. In interviews, some newcomers admitted to listening to his Live at the Apollo sets on repeat, studying the rhythm, the pauses, the way Evans wielded silence as effectively as a punchline.

But perhaps the most significant part of his legacy is the way he brought wit into unexpected spaces. His work on Radio 4 programs like The News Quiz demonstrated that comedy and current affairs need not be in opposition. By weaving satire into discussions of politics and economics, Evans not only entertained but also encouraged audiences to think critically about the world around them. In doing so, he helped shape a genre of comedy that was not only reactive but also reflective — comedy that aimed not just to make people laugh, but to make them consider why they were laughing in the first place.

Outside the stage lights, Evans' influence extended into writing and commentary. His essays and public appearances often revealed the same careful observation and intellectual curiosity that fueled his stand-up. These forays into more serious domains underscored what fans already suspected: Simon Evans was, above all else, a thinker. Comedy was his medium, but insight was his true message.

It would be easy to view Evans' career as a steady climb toward recognition, but his legacy is more complex than that. There were, of course, moments of controversy. Comedy rarely thrives without a measure of risk, and Evans occasionally courted criticism for the sharpness of his views. Yet these moments only added to the richness of his story. They demonstrated that Evans wasn't afraid to provoke thought, even if it meant sparking debate. In a cultural climate that often prizes caution, Evans' willingness to speak with conviction was itself a legacy.

Looking back, one sees a career defined by choices — choices to embrace intelligence rather than pander, to trust that audiences could keep up with his references and follow his logic. Those choices paid off, carving a unique space for him in British comedy. He may not have chased stardom in the same way some of his peers did, but what he achieved was perhaps more lasting: respect. Respect from audiences, from critics, and most tellingly, from other comedians.

Even as the comedy landscape evolved — as digital platforms democratized access and younger performers experimented with TikTok sketches or Instagram reels — Evans' style retained its place. He represented something steady, a reminder of comedy's roots in live performance, in the shared experience of people gathered together, listening and laughing in real time. His legacy, then, was not only in the words he spoke but in the moments he created: a theatre buzzing with anticipation, the pause before the punchline, the eruption of laughter that felt both intimate and universal.

For Evans, comedy was never just a career. It was a way of engaging with the world. It was a

THE SIMON EVANS BIOGRAPHY

way of dissecting contradictions, of pulling threads loose to reveal the absurdity beneath. He gave his audiences more than entertainment; he gave them a way of seeing. And in that way of seeing — sharp, wry, deeply observant — lies the true legacy of Simon Evans.

As his story folds into the broader narrative of British comedy, Evans stands as proof that intelligence and laughter are not mutually exclusive. His career reminds us that comedy can be cerebral without being inaccessible, that a joke can both tickle and teach. And perhaps most importantly, it shows that one man, armed with nothing but a microphone, can hold up a mirror to society and, with a well-placed punchline, help us all laugh at what we see.

THE SIMON EVANS BIOGRAPHY

Simon Evans may one day take his final bow, as all performers must. But his voice — measured, precise, and unmistakably his own — will echo on, preserved in recordings, remembered in routines, and carried forward in the comedians he inspired. His is a legacy not just of laughter, but of thought, of courage, and of an unwavering belief in the power of words to change the way we feel, the way we think, and sometimes, even the way we live.

Conclusion

The arc of Simon Evans' life in comedy has been one of persistence, sharp intelligence, and a refusal to bend to fashion. Where some comedians pivot with every cultural tide, Evans carved a place for himself by holding fast to a brand of wit that prizes craft, intellect, and observation over easy applause. It is this consistency, coupled with his ability to skewer the absurdities of modern life with both precision and charm, that has earned him a lasting place in British comedy.

From the small clubs and open-mic nights where he first tested his material, Evans brought a confidence that seemed to belong to someone who had already lived many lives. His voice—both literally, with its crisp diction, and figuratively, with its distinct perspective—set him apart from the start. Where others leaned into slapstick or populist jokes, Evans offered something more refined. He wasn't just trying to get a laugh; he was trying to provoke thought. This was the foundation of his reputation: a comedian who trusted the intelligence of his audience.

Over the decades, Evans became more than just a fixture on stage. His work on radio, particularly with *Simon Evans Goes to Market*, introduced him to an audience beyond the clubs and theatres. Here, his knack for blending humor with complex subjects came to the forefront. Economics, politics, and philosophy were not the easiest topics to package for entertainment, but Evans made them accessible. He had the rare ability to turn an analysis of inflation or the housing market into a wry observation that left listeners both laughing and thinking. That synthesis of depth and levity became his hallmark.

Of course, the life of a comedian is never without obstacles. Evans' comedy often courted debate, sometimes controversy. His willingness to critique sacred cows of modern culture meant that he occasionally found himself at odds with prevailing sentiments. Yet, he did not retreat. Instead, he leaned further into his persona: the witty contrarian, the man willing to say what others hesitated to. This courage—tempered always by his dry humor—made him a distinctive voice in an increasingly crowded field.

THE SIMON EVANS BIOGRAPHY

What truly elevates Evans' story, however, is not just his comedy but his resilience. The circuit is unforgiving; trends shift, audiences evolve, and countless comedians fall away. Evans endured. He adapted when necessary but without abandoning the qualities that made him unique. This balancing act—remaining true to one's voice while still growing as an artist—is no small feat. For Evans, it was a lifelong practice, akin to a craftsman polishing his work again and again until it gleamed.

In his personal life, too, Evans carried the weight of his public persona with grace. Those who know him speak of a man who is deeply thoughtful, curious, and occasionally as sharp in private conversation as he is on stage. Yet beneath the wit is a person attuned to the absurdities of human existence not just as material for jokes, but as reflections of the shared human condition. That empathy—sometimes hidden behind the armor of sarcasm—remains one of the undercurrents of his comedy.

As the years have passed, Evans has come to embody a rare kind of comedian: one who appeals both to the intellect and the funny bone, one whose material feels timeless even as the world changes rapidly around it. Audiences may come expecting to laugh, but they leave with something more—a perspective, an insight, a subtle nudge to think differently about the everyday. That is a legacy far richer than applause alone.

Looking back across his journey, one can trace the threads that made Simon Evans who he is.

The curiosity sparked in childhood, the years of honing his voice in small venues, the breakthroughs in radio and television, the risks taken in pushing against the grain, and the triumphs earned through sheer perseverance—all these moments form a mosaic of a life devoted to comedy. And through it all, his humor has remained a steady companion, illuminating not only the quirks of the world but also the enduring resilience of laughter itself.

It is easy to measure a comedian's success by ticket sales, TV appearances, or the length of their Wikipedia page. But the truer measure lies in the memories they leave behind: the audience members who recall a line years later, the laughter that echoes in minds long after the show ends, the quiet comfort of knowing that even the most complex or frustrating realities of life can be approached with a smile. By this measure, Simon Evans has succeeded in abundance.

His career tells us something important about comedy itself. It is not always about chasing trends or pandering to the broadest crowd. Sometimes, it is about standing firm in one's perspective, trusting that there are audiences who crave wit over whimsy, insight over noise. Evans exemplifies that truth. His work is proof that there will always be space for comedians who bring more than punchlines—they bring a way of seeing the world.

As the curtain falls on this story, one is left with the sense that Evans' greatest gift is not just his humor but his integrity. In a profession where it is easy to compromise for the sake of exposure or success, he remained authentic. He understood that comedy, at its best, is not simply about entertainment but about connection—the bond forged between performer and audience through shared laughter, even over difficult truths.

Simon Evans may never have chased the glitz of celebrity with the same vigor as others in his field, but he carved a career of substance, intelligence, and durability. His wit has become part of the landscape of British comedy, not in the flashy headlines but in the enduring memory of those who laughed with him. And in the end, that is the true measure of his legacy.

For those who step into the world of comedy, Evans' journey offers a lesson: the path may not always be glamorous, but if one holds fast to authenticity, sharpens the craft, and respects the intelligence of one's audience, the rewards are immeasurable. For audiences, his legacy is simpler yet profound—the reminder that laughter and thought are not opposites but allies, and that in the hands of the right comedian, they can illuminate the world together.

And so, Simon Evans' story does not end with the final applause of a show or the closing credits of a radio series. It lives on in the echoes of laughter, in the raised eyebrows of recognition, and in the timelessness of wit well-delivered. For in the end, what Simon Evans truly gave his audiences was not just comedy—it was clarity, perspective, and the lasting joy of seeing life anew, one perfectly measured punchline at a time.

Printed in Dunstable, United Kingdom